Bede's Bird

©Kara Louise Hughes
2019

All rights reserved. No part of this book may be reproduced or transmitted in any form or by any means, including electronic or mechanical including photocopying or recording or by any information storage or retrieval system without permission in writing from the author.

Bede's Bird: A Collection Of Poems

Kara Hughes

For Edwin
Whose encouragement and thoughtfulness,
Has always been my inspiration.

Contents

Chanard 1
Three Haiku 2
The Stars 3
Autopsy 4
Cychwyniad 5
Dathliadau 6
Mermaid 7
We Are Wales 8
Epithalamion 11
Prothalamion 13
Messenger 15
Passing Time 16
Ashurah 17
Bede's Bird 18
Thalassa 19
Apellation 20
River 21
My Tree 22
Bahrain 23
November 24
Seven Days 25
A Song for Thetis 27
Camping 29
The Loss 30
Come With Me 31
The Slipper 32

Chanard

Tinsel tied to the hook,
And swung out across the stern
Of the yacht, watching
The sparkling lure as it spun
Under the dark, foaming ocean.

A hoary shape shooting
To catch the glittering bait
And then the fight,
As we pulled the shining quarry,
From the ocean depths,

Silver, white flecked foam, midnight blue
Combine as we haul the beast
Into the vessel's cockpit,
Heart thumping in my ears as I stumble
To fetch the gaff to despatch the fish.

Three Haiku

Ride the dawn with me
Zephyrs across golden fields
Herald the new day

Verdant leaves shimmer
Their greenness a harbinger
Of autumn's decay

Pale apple blossom
Hangs over the wooden fence
Summer brings sweet fruit

The Stars

I remember the summoning stars,
That held me in thrall
From the first night I looked up,
Blazing brightness across black velvet heaven
Diamonds scattered on sultry satin
And through them, the cutthroat cloud
Of the Milky Way,
Showing me the path home.

We do not see these burning orbs
As they truly are, we see them as they were
Thousands of years ago
So this scintillating star
Blazing blue-white in the darkness
May not now even exist
Having gone supernova,
Hundreds of eons ago.

Autopsy

I would like to witness,
The death of a star.
To see for one brief, agonizing moment
An explosion that lights up the heavens,
Destroying planets.

But in the debris from this sun
Lie the seeds of another unborn universe
And when our sun goes nova – as one day it must,
In that ending will also be
A new beginning.

Cychwyniad[1]

I remember the very first day
I saw this place of learning
From a sky of deep cerulean blue
A daffodil yellow sun shone down
On this University.
And I knew with a sudden sharp clarity
Here was where I wanted to study
For here I felt as though a need
Had been assuaged
Even though I never knew what it was
Save that Lampeter
Granted it in some strange way.

Dathliadau[2]

I return to this place, my *alma mater*
Half-familiar, half-stranger and wonder
If ghosts walk these cloisters
As they do in my memory.
I see us walking down to lectures,
Across the quad to the Chapel
I think there are ghosts here, quiet spirits
Not seen at midnight down gloomy cloisters
But visible in shafts of sunlight
Making dust motes sparkle –
And memories shine like pure gold.

Mermaid

*This was my attempt at a 'Paradelle' a form created by the poet Billy Elliot to parody the Villanelle

I remember floating in green incandescence
I remember floating in green incandescence
Phosphorescent fire around my fingers
Phosphorescent fire around my fingers
In incandescence floating I remember
Around my fingers green phosphorescent fire.

Diving into that wine-dark ocean
Diving into that wine dark ocean
I surface lucific with seawater
I surface lucific with seawater
Diving I surface with seawater
Lucific into that wine-dark ocean.

Glowing I swim against the black tide
Glowing I swim against the black tide
The moon milk-pale in the heavens
The moon milk-pale in the heavens
Moon glowing I swim in the heavens
Milk-pale against the black tide.

Diving into phosphorescent green
With incandescence I swim that fire
Floating milk-pale in the heavens
Remember the moon in the black tide
Around my fingers wine-dark ocean,
I surface lucific against glowing seawater.

We Are Wales

From Snowdon's granite peaks, across the Menai Straits
To Môn Mam Cymru[3], down past Longshanks'[4] Castles,
Past Swallow Falls, past the Mountain Railways.
We are Gwenfrewi[5] and Holywell,
And older voices echo down the years –
Before Christianity, before God
A time of Druid and Bard - of the great Bear himself,
Who strode, Orion-like up the sky
His flaming sword drawn to subdue invaders.
We are Taliesin, The Bard,
We are Myrddin Emrys,
Bardsey calls us too,
The island of twenty thousand saints,
Then onto St. Illtyd's place,
The first university in Britain
(Although it was really Wales.)
Here Dewi Sant studied, and, according to legend,
Maenwyn also, before he was taken by God
To teach the Irish. (We know him as St. Patrick.)
Then Tintern and the Abbey
Serenely defying the centuries
Then on to Llandewi Brefi where Saint David,
Preached and the Holy Spirit
Landed on his shoulder as a Dove
Up to Llanbeder Pont Steffan and on to Tyddewi,
St. Davids, the Great Cathedral
(Built so that it could not be seen by invaders),
We are Saint Cadfan, patron saint of warriors,
Christmas Evans, George Fox
And the man who opened the heart of a nation,

Evan Roberts.
But we bear *dwysder* also, and the pall of Aberfan
Still hangs over all of Wales.
Yet we are the Dragon, *Y Ddraig Goch*,
Who keeps still the guarded watch on Cymru.
And now we rise on wings –
To show that Cymru has not lost who she is,
That we are King Arthur,
Owen ap Grufuyydd Fychan, Prince and True King of Wales,
We are kingdom and cantref,
Max Boyce, Rugby and Cardiff Arms Park
Our heritage is always with us
In every hymn we sing, from Calon Lân to Cwm Rhondda
We are Wales and Cymru still
'Tis Longshanks who lies dead.

Epithalamion

May this Spring day dawn bright and clear
The Church bells in every steeple ring
A man and woman have come here
And the whole of creation shall sing!
Full glasses we will to heaven raise,
Celebrate this day with both of you
With songs and psalms and hymns of praise.
For today two lives shall be joined as one
Beneath the moon and under the sun.

The sun has risen and her daffodil rays
Have poured in through your window pane
Bride awake! Your room is set ablaze
With light and suddenly nothing seems the same
For today, you marry and become a wife
As you and your love stand before God and Man
And begin, together a whole new life.
This day, two lives are joined as one,
Beneath the moon and under the sun

Cymru's rugged warriors with eyes of steel
And gentle Bridesmaids with orchids crowned
Demonstrate your prowess and with zeal
Bring Bride and Groom to be bound –
As husband and wife in this Holy Place
One to the other within these Abbey walls
And may God grant your union Grace.
For two lives will be joined as one,
Beneath the moon and under the sun.

Beneath this cerulean cup of the sky
As man and woman, hand in hand
Let Love and Happiness mystically tie
Each to the other, and as you stand
Happy and dazed, side by side
We say our farewells and depart,
Our nation overwhelmed with joy and pride.
Leaving you both joined as one,
Beneath the moon and under the sun.

Prothalamion

Let Aeolus, Poseidon's Son, bright and fair
Lord of the winds, gather these breezes together,
Boreas, from the Northern climes most frozen air
Eurus, from the exotic, oriental eastern lands
Notus, god of the damp and foggy south,
And Zephyrus, god of the western sands
Bring them all together on this day
To send forth to all the gladdening news,
That this day may all the immortals sing
That the woods may answer and my Echo ring.

Helios in his chariot, by Apollo's horses drawn
Across the heavens, and now the daffodil sun
Streams through your window on this most joyful morn
Bride awake! Leave now your solitary bed
For today you marry and become a wife
And before God and man you will be Wed.
Join with the one who holds your heart
And become to him both lover and friend
The universe will take pause at your crowning
And the woods will answer and my Echo ring.

Let the Bridesmaids come with hearts aflame
Pride of your nation bring glad spirits with you
And with your touch all mystic creatures tame
To keep the Pwca and Unseelie Court
Away from this bright couple on this day,
That their hateful nature come to naught.
And ask the Seelie Court that they may grant
Blessings and munificence on these two.
For this glorious princess and her princeling
That the woods may answer and my Echo ring.

Rugged, russet men with eyes of steel
Ancient Warriors from England's shores
Saxon, Celt, Norman whose noble zeal
Is etched into the soil of this land
Bring the bridegroom to this Holy Kirk
That he may be joined hand in hand
Beneath the heavens with his Bride.
That your new life will begin flowering
That the woods may answer, and my Echo ring.

Beneath this cerulean bowl of the sky
You both will be joined as one
Love and Holiness mystically tie
One to the other so they as one heart
Stand together through all assaults
That might attempt to tear them apart.
Yet don't forget to tell the Bees,
That your diligence gain reward
On you The Thriae shower a honeyed blessing
And the woods shall answer, and my Echo ring.

Messenger

Clink of coffee cup;
Hiss of cappucino machine,
Making white frothed lattes –
Mingling with the movement
Of shoppers, as the Angel Gabriel
Walks down Dudley Street.

Few recognise him – after all,
He is wingless, carries no sword,
But one or two catch a glimpse,
Eyes of blazing golden fire
An aura of electricity around him
As for a moment he seems to have a halo.

Then they blink, shrug, move on –
Turning their attention back,
To the tawdry, cheap outlets,
Never caring or even knowing
For a moment, a part of the Divine
Walks unnoticed in their midst.

Passing Time

This glorious summer will not last,
Too soon the golden harvests fall –
And all this wonder be in the past.

We humans remain always outclassed,
By nature's ability to enthrall
This glorious summer will not last.

Lucious fruits their bounty vast,
Heavy with this season's windfall
And all this wonder be in the past

This heavenly beauty unsurpassed,
Will fade away to Autumn's pall,
And all this wonder be in the past

The earth continues to give unasked,
But does not think her gift banal,
This glorious summer will not last.

Memories should not become a ghast –
To hold us prisoners in Time's thrall,
This glorious summer will not last,
And all this wonder be in the past.

Ashurah

'Come to the roof,' he said, 'Watch,
But make no noise.'
And we stood – a silent group
As the young men, half-naked
With swords and chains
Began to beat and cut themselves
Until the blood ran freely down lithe bodies,
Staining their clothes and dripping
Onto the tarmac.
And I stared with a ten year old's
Fascination and horror,
As they danced, flailed and injured
Themselves. To mourn the death of
The grandson of the Prophet Muhammed.

Bede's Bird

The present life of man, O king, seems to me, like to the swift flight of a sparrow through the room wherein you sit at supper in winter, with your commanders and ministers, and a good fire in the midst, whilst the storms of rain and snow prevail abroad; the sparrow, I say, flying in at one door, and immediately out at another, whilst he is within, is safe from the wintry storm; but after a short space of fair weather, he immediately vanishes out of your sight, into the dark winter from which he had emerged. So this life of man appears for a short space, but of what went before, or what is to follow, we are utterly ignorant. If, therefore, this new doctrine contains something more certain, it seems justly to deserve to be followed. **Bede: Ecclesiastical History of the English People**

We are all Bede's bird -
Although this may seem quite absurd.
A sparrow shears through a golden hall,
Too fast to brake; too fast to stall -
Into the dark and frigid air -
And vanishes, we know not where.
Others ask, 'Where does the sparrow fly?'
Some say to live; some say to die.
Cynics say there's no bird at all,
Nor priest, nor feast, nor banquet hall,
But all is just a pleasant dream,
Of things hoped for, and yet unseen,
Yet in my travels I have heard,
Brave men have died to spread The Word
That we are all Bede's bird.

Thalassa

When the men in front reached the summit and caught sight of the sea there was great shouting. Xenophon and the rearguard heard it and thought that there were enemies attacking in the front. However, the shouting got louder and drew nearer. Those who were constantly going forward started running towards the men in front, who kept on shouting. And the more there were of them, the more shouting there was. It looked then as though this was something of considerable importance. So Xenophon mounted his horse, and taking Lycus and the cavalry with him, rode forward to give support. And quite soon they heard the soldiers shouting out thalassa, thalassa, 'The sea!, the sea!' and passing the word down the column.
Xenophon The Persian Expedition

I remember the grey sea first, before
My salt-caked hair; or my hands
Raw from hauling the boat's sheets.

It is the cold sea first; before the wind
Catching the spinnaker, my father's voice
Asking 'Ready about?' Waiting for my nod.

Blue, green, grey, phosphorescent waves
Are always with me before boat or yacht or island
It is always the sea.

Despite my years of sailing; Toppers, Lasers, Fireballs
Whenever I recall the Middle East,
It is always the ocean first.

Apellation

I was named for the Hurricane,
The wild wind that whips across oceans
Causing death and destruction
And for years I loathed it –
Hated the connotations my name evoked,
That people thought me wild and crazy,
Because of my name.

But in recent years I have come
To a kind of peace,
With my name; revelling in its
Uniqueness, its scarcity
And even though today, my rubric
Is not so unusual – I take pride in the knowledge
I was the first.

River

A pulsing, foaming, cascading heart,
Tumbles cold and fierce and free –
From the snow mountains of its birth
Meandering slowly across the landscape,
Becoming steady, pumping arteries
Turgid brown waters toiling towards
The open ocean, becoming tributaries,
Veins, capillaries, forming an estuary
Flowing across a verdant landscape,
To spill nutrient rich seed into the sea.

My Tree

Kipling wrote, 'Oak, Ash, Thorn are the Trees of England,'
Oak for ships, steadfast – tall and sturdy – enduring.
Ash for the Vikings – The World Tree, Yggdrasil –
Druids made their wands from the Ash Tree –
And finally the Thorn or Rowan. The Sacred Three
Of the Druids and of Faerie. And there are other Trees
The Yew – *taxus baccata* – most noble of trees,
Longbow wood; defender of Crecy, and of Agincourt
The weapon of Robin Hood. But none of these is my tree.

My tree grows in sandy soil – against a sky of dazzling blue
And bears, as its fruit, bunches of huge ochre drupes,
My tree is the *Phoenix dactylifera* – the date palm
When I was young I lived in a villa
Within its walls there stood at least thirty date palms,
I remember the huge bunches, like enormous yellow grapes,
Hanging next to the cooker – a gift from the labourers
Who would line up every year outside the gate
To beg permission to harvest the crop.

Bahrain

'Blessed is the land of Dilmun'
Gilgamesh, King of Uruk travelled here
From his relative, Uta Napishtim
Who knew the secret of Dilmun,
That it was the Garden of Eden, doubly blessed
With clear fountains and the gift of eternal youth.

'Blessed is the land of Dilmun'
Could it have been this small kingdom
That was the centre of the world?
The fabled Paradise were all life dwelt
In Peace? Where the lion did not kill
Nor the wolf snatch the lamb?

'Blessed is the land of Dilmun'
Still I think about the fate of Gilgamesh
Who came seeking everlasting life,
But fell asleep and lost the magic plant
To a passing serpent, making snakes immortal
And Gilgamesh saddened, returned to Uruk.

November

A wet-dog morning
Mist rising from rain soaked grass,
Seeping into the walkers on the heath
Leeching colour from the world.

Seven Days

Monday – Moon's Day, Artemis, Goddess of the Hunt
Hecate, Goddess of the Midnight, The Dark Moon
Sina, Protector of those who travel by Night –
Who paddled her canoe to that shining orb –
And decided to stay.

Tuesday – Tiw's Day, Tyr's Day -
God of Justice, Law and Victory –
Who lost his hand to Fenrir, Loki's son,
When the gods bound this wolf against the end of the world -
Ragnarok.

Wednesday – Woden's day, Odin's Day,
Odin of the Ravens, Master of Ecstasy –
Odin, All–Father, One–Eyed, Wanderer –
Who hanged himself on Yggdrasil,
To gain wisdom.

Thursday – Thor's Day, Thor of the Thunder –
Wielder of Mjölnir, Rider of the Lightning,
Half- god, Odinsson, Strongest of Warriors –
Doomed to die by the Midgard Serpent
Jormungand.

Friday – Frigg's Day, Queen of Asgard,
Wife to Odin, crowned with Heron plumes –
Mistress of Silence, Goddess of Beauty and Love,
Dweller in the Halls of Mists –
Fensalir.

Saturday – Saturn's Day, the Roman god Saturn,
Kronos his Greek name, first of the Titans,
God of the Harvests and the Seasons –
Oldest and Wisest of them all – enduring
Father of Truth.

Sunday – *dies Solis*. The day of the Sun
Holiday and Holy Day – both together –
A day of rest from work, a day of celebration,
By decree of the first Christian Emperor of Rome
Constantine I.

A Song for Thetis

A reply to Thetis from the book 'The Song of Achilles'

Thetis, I would say to you –
You could not make your son a god –
But man has made him immortal –
When men speak of Achilles –
They will remember one who blazed
Like a comet – who shone
Like a thousand splendid Suns –
Who stood before the walls of Troy,
Who honoured his oath, firm of purpose –
A warrior amongst men.

When Bards sing your son's name –
Others will join the Chorus
Odysseus, King of Ithaca –
Agamemnon, Menelaus, Hector,
Priam, Paris, even the foolish Helen.
And the oft forgotten Patroclus –
All will have their names sung
To the firmament for evermore –
That men may know of their deeds
And remember their glory.

Thetis, the gods are dead –
Gone, dwindled to nothingness,
Their names only recited in story,
They have given way to a better God,
A God who does not seek vengeance –
But Justice, Humility and Mercy.
Thetis, it is written – that a man is not dead –
Until his name has been forgotten.
And, Thetis, your son's name
Will never be forgotten.

Camping

I set the lantern on the rock,
And sit while my parents
Using the car's headlights,
Put up the tent. The blue white light,
Shows a path, across the rocky desert floor.

Androctonus crassicauda. Man-killer
Fattail scorpion. Black in the lantern light
I watch as it lifts tiny pincers in salute and is gone
Scurrying across the path
Seeking darkness and stealth.

Moths buzz around the lamp,
Too fast to see clearly or identify
Confusing false light for the moon.
And then a flash of green -
Resting on the glass panels.

Mantis religiosa Praying mantid.
Prehistoric green - found only in nature.
Amazed at this delicate, ferocious creature,
I stare, transfixed and repulsed
With the eyes of a child.

The Loss

Always the wind blows from the sea
Denting the iris
Salt spray stinging the eyes
Memories of tears.
The greasy, green sea rolls
And scoops up gravel in his paws,
I grasp your hand tightly –
And wonder if you understand
Daddy isn't coming home.

Did others stand like this?
Watching the horizon for ships
Even when all hope was lost?
And what of Sarah who knew with certainty
Her French lover would not come back
And that she was damned.
But continued her lonely vigil
Should I emulate her and do the same,
Knowing, as she knew, that there will be no return.

No! I shall endure
As the sea itself endures
To roll and roar forever,
For in my dreams you come to me,
Your skin white as the cuttlefish,
Your fingers translucent seashells
On your breath I smell the salt,
And in your voice I hear –
The thunder of the waves.

Come With Me

When the sun is a quenched dragon's eye,
And the grass stands pilum sharp
On a December morning -
I will show you the hibernating dormouse
An auburn fox trotting through the mist
A fat rabbit in his jaws.

In this frost filled world
When the universe seems asleep,
You will see the world open
Before you, showing the petals
Of a brilliant, fragile flower
Held in sparkling crystal.

Even in this torpid season,
In the cold, crisp snow-threatening void
As your breath condenses in frozen air,
See Starlings in their murmurations,
Making hieroglyphs in winter sky
Dancing to a music we cannot hear.

The Slipper

There was one slipper by the garden gate,
Glistening blue in the dew-wet grass,
And I wondered if some sprite
Had lost it on her way home –
From a fairy ball, or it had simply slipped
From her hand when she removed
Her high-heeled shoes, to quietly tiptoe home
Without disturbing anyone.

And I thought about taking it home,
To finally prove the existence of little people
But as I watched, it vanished
Dissolving into the foliage around it,
Until there was only the turf
Birdsong and me.

Index Of First Lines

Always the wind blows from the sea 30
A pulsing, foaming, cascading heart 21
A wet-dog morning 24
'Blessed is the land of Dilmun' 23
Clink of coffee cup 15
'Come to the roof,' he said, 'Watch 17
From Snowdon's granite peaks, across the Menai Straits 9
I remember floating in green incandescence 7
I remember the grey sea first, before 19
I remember the summoning stars 3
I remember the very first day 5
I return to this place, my *alma mater* 6
I set the lantern on the rock 29
I was named for the Hurricane 20
I would like to witness 4
Kipling wrote, 'Oak, Ash, Thorn are the Trees of England ... 22
Let Aeolus, Poseidon's Son, bright and fair 13
May this Spring day dawn bright and clear 11
Monday – Moon's Day, Artemis, Goddess of the Hunt 25
Ride the dawn with me 2
There was one slipper by the garden gate 32
Thetis, I would say to you – 27
This glorious summer will not last 16
Tinsel tied to the hook 1
We are all Bede's bird - 18
When the sun is a quenched dragon's eye 31

Biography

Kara Hughes holds a BA (Hons) English/Theology from the University of Wales, Lampeter and an MA in Creative Writing from Trinity College, Carmathen. She has been writing since she was ten years old and lived for almost twenty years in the Middle East. Many of her poems have been previously published in *Carillon* and *Dial 174* (now sadly discontinued.) Two poems in this collection *Bede's Bird* and *Thalassa* were entered in the 2018 Perton Show and *Bede's Bird* won the CAP Literature Cup.

---

[1] Means 'Start or Beginning' in Welsh
[2] Means 'Celebration' in Welsh
[3] Anglesey
[4] Edward I
[5] St. Winifred

Printed in Dunstable, United Kingdom